GREENACRE ON THE PISCATAQUA.

ANNA JOSEPHINE INGERSOLL.

NEW YORK:
THE ALLIANCE PUBLISHING COMPANY,
"LIFE" BUILDING.

Windham Press is committed to bringing the lost cultural heritage of ages past into the 21st century through high-quality reproductions of original, classic printed works at affordable prices.

This book has been carefully crafted to utilize the original images of antique books rather than error-prone OCR text. This also preserves the work of the original typesetters of these classics, unknown craftsmen who laid out the text, often by hand, of each and every page you will read. Their subtle art involving judgment and interaction with the text is in many ways superior and more human than the mechanical methods utilized today, and gave each book a unique, hand-crafted feel in its text that connected the reader organically to the art of bindery and book-making.

We think these benefits are worth the occasional imperfection resulting from the age of these books at the time of scanning, and their vintage feel provides a connection to the past that goes beyond the mere words of the text.

As bibliophiles, we are always seeking perfection in our work, so please notify us of any errors in this book by emailing us at corrections@windhampress.com. Our team is motivated to correct errors quickly so future customers are better served. Our mission is to raise the bar of quality for reprinted works by a focus on detail and quality over mass production.

To peruse our catalog of carefully curated classic works, please visit our online store at www.windhampress.com.

GREENACRE ON THE PISCATAQUA.

TO the traveler speeding through New England on the Eastern Division of the Boston & Maine Railroad there is no hint of any special attraction at the plain little station of Eliot. A drive of three miles takes you past thrifty homes, with meadows reaching to the broad, swift Piscataqua, and through stretches of dense woods down to the river bank, where almost at the entrance to Long Reach Bay stands the Greenacre Inn. It is a quiet spot, with gently sloping banks, and off to the west lies a long meadow with its fringe of apple trees and birches reflected in the waters of the bay. There is a sense of space and distance, a limitless expanse of sky, a broad sweep of river and bay with the distant low-lying banks, and far beyond, ever changing in hue against the sunset sky, range the foothills of the White Mountains. With the going down of the sun a golden bridge spans the waters glowing and radiant at our feet.

Once there was a desperate struggle here; men fought for their lives, while women and children hurried for shelter over the fields to the garrison house with its high stockade. There are yet signs to be seen of this old house, and in the fields about the plough has turned up many an arrow-head. As late as 1747 the men of this district carried firearms to church.

Down in the hollow below the Inn where the apple trees and locusts bloom, there was a large ship-yard in the fifties, where the keel of many a good ship was laid. The fleetest sailing vessel of her day, The Nightingale, built to carry Jenny Lind

Goldsmith back to Sweden, floated out on the tide from these cool, green shores. She never fulfilled her purpose, and years after was captured by the government with a cargo of wretched human beings bound for the slave market.

The Eliot of to-day is a quiet farming town of 1,500 inhabitants, lying for six miles along the banks of the beautiful Piscataqua, just over the Maine border line, four miles from Portsmouth, New Hampshire. There are three or four churches, a grocery store or two, and one hotel, Greenacre Inn, built ten years ago by a company of enterprising Eliot people. The Inn, a small house holding about one hundred people, was for a few years a resort for Bostonians. Here John Greenleaf Whittier came, drawing about him a circle of friends.

In 1893, that wonderful year, when, through the World's Parliament of Religions, men were brought to a recognition of the fundamental points of contact in the religions of the world, Miss Sarah J. Farmer, only daughter of Moses G. Farmer, the inventor, conceived the idea of continuing at Eliot, Maine, her birthplace, the movement inaugurated at Chicago. She determined to form a centre at the Greenacre Inn, where thinking men and women, reaching out to help their fellows through means tried and untried, might find an audience recognizing not alone revealed truth, but truth in the process of revelation. It was believed that for those of different faiths, different nationalities, different training, the points of contact might be found, the great underlying principles — the oneness of truth, the brotherhood of man; that to the individual this spot might mean the opening door to freedom, the tearing down of walls of prejudice and superstition. The teachers and lecturers on this broad platform were to give their services without remuneration. There was no endowment fund, and the expense of their transportation and entertainment was met through voluntary contributions. Where else in the world's history do we find such another cornerstone?

In July, 1894, Greenacre Inn was opened to guests under Miss Farmer's management. Less expensive accommodations were to be had in the farm houses about. An encampment of tents pitched on the river bank, over in the meadow where the old garrison house stood, gave those desiring it the freedom of open-air life. Although six miles from the sea, the tide rises high at Eliot, and the opportunities for salt-water bathing are fine.

The great lecture tent seating three hundred was raised just beyond the stone wall of the meadow. The afternoon of the third day of July had been appointed for the opening exercises of the Greenacre Lecture Course, and only a few had gathered. Mrs. Ole Bull, of Cambridge, delivered the address of welcome. At the close of the exercises we stood with heads uncovered to raise the stars and stripes. For days the sky had been dark and lowering, but as we sang "The Battle Hymn of the Republic," the clouds parted a little and a flood of sunshine illuminated the scene. It was with every man's hand to the rope that the flag of our country went up, and under it there floated for the first time over these green fields a white flag with the legend "Peace" upon it.

The first year brought such men as Henry Wood, Frank B. Sanborn, Edward Everett Hale, O. C. Dolbear, Lewis G. Janes, Ralph Waldo Trine, Vivekananda, W. J. Colville and others, and they have continued to come; such women as Ursula Gestefeld, Helen Van-Anderson, Josephine Locke, Abby Morton Diaz. The programs of the succeeding years have added many names of value—J. Vance Cheney, John Angus MacVannel, William Norman Guthrie, John S. Clark, S. T. Rorer, Edna D. Cheney, William Ordway Partridge, Samuel Walter Foss, Carroll D. Wright, Samuel Richard Fuller, Mary A. Livermore, Emily Perkins Stetson, Elizabeth Boynton Harbert, Edwin Elwell, Lucia Ames Mead, Helen M. Cole, Kate Tannett Woods, Edwin Markham, George D. Herron, Julia Osgood, Edward S. Morse, William Lloyd Garrison, W. T. Harris, H. W. Stetson, Lyman C. Newell, Egbert Morse Chesley, Sara G. Farwell, Thomas Ryan, Mary Lowe Dickerson, John J. Enneking, Frederick Reed, Filmore Moore, Mary Proctor, Mitchell Tyng, Ellen Crosby, Helen Weil, Josiah Strong, Henry Hoyt Moore, W. H. Tolman, Thomas Van Ness, T. Yanaguchi, Ethel Puffer, Rachel Foster Avery, John Bowles, Benjamin F. Trueblood, Neal Dow,

J. T. Trowbridge, Alfred Norton, Ellen A. Richardson, Arthur Dow, Lysander Dickerman, Sadie American, Lilian Whiting, Ernest F. Fenollosa, Theodore F. Wright, C. A. L. Totten, Caroline H. Hindobro, Amanda Deyo.

A wonderful sifting process has been going on through these years, working silently for the most part, eliminating the man with the personal "ism," the "fad," the so-called crank, and sometimes finding, in the abundance of what the world calls chaff, the kernel of wheat.

Since the first season the order of the day has been much the same. At nine o'clock devotional exercises in the lecture tent, and then the leisurely trooping up over the hills to the Lysekloster pines, where, in pleasant weather, the platform of the morning is a carpet of pine needles under a great pine tree. On rainy days, the morning lectures are given under a tent in the pines, and the afternoon lectures during the last few years have been given in the new lecture hall, The Eirenion; but on bright days we listen to music and the lecture of the day in the great tent, with its sides wide open to the river, and with all the life and freedom of the summer about. At sunset there is a quiet hour in the tent, and once or twice a week a musical program. The music school, under the direction of Miss Mary H. Burnham, has been an important factor in the Greenacre work.

In 1896 the general lecture course was divided into conferences beginning Sunday afternoon and continuing one week, and a Nature School out in the woods and fields was formed for the children, under Daniel Batchellor and Melvin G. Dodge. In this same year, a school of comparative religions was founded under the directorship of Doctor Lewis

G. Janes, director of the Cambridge Conferences.

This school has been one of the strongest features of the Greenacre Lecture Course. The sessions have been held during August under the pines. The motive has been comparative study and never propagation of doctrine. During the four years Lewis G. Janes, director of the school, has given a number of valuable lectures upon various subjects. This last summer's work held nothing more broadly helpful and suggestive than Dr. Janes's course upon social science and applied religion. The Swamis Vivekananda, Saradananda and Abhedananda have in turn expounded the profound philosophy of the Vedanta.

The history, ethics and theology of the Talmud were presented by Rabbi Joseph Silverman; the teaching of Jesus by Jean du Buy, and the religion and philosophy of the Jains by Virchand R. Gandhi; Nathaniel Schmidt of Cornell University gave this year an exceptionally interesting course on ancient Hebrew philosophers. A brilliantly dramatic presentation of the sacred and religious customs in Mohammedan countries was given by the Syrian Shehadi Abd-Allah Shehadi. From the standpoint of the Christianized Hindu, T. B. Pandian described the social conditions and missionary work in India. Lack of space alone forbids the mention of many other valuable contributions to this program. The discussions after the lectures are carried on with a calm, judicial temper, a courtesy, a respect for the opinions of others, an evident desire for "Truth and not for victory," that cannot fail to make them educational.

As we glance over the programs of the years we find Edward Griggs on "The Art of Living," Smith Baker's morning classes on developmental psychology with their wonderful lessons in life, W. S. Tomlin's talks on music, E. P. Powell on "The Evolution of a Home," Hezekiah Butterworth on "The Art of Story Telling." Francis B. Hornbrook talks on Browning, B. O. Flower on Marcus Aurelius and Epictetus, W. D. Howells reads his "Etruria," Annie Besant lectures on "Immortality," C. H. A. Bjerregaard on "The Mystic Life," John Fiske on "The Cosmic Roots of Self-sacrifice," Lester A. Ward on "The Real Moral Evolution," Joseph LeConte on "The Relation of Biology to Philosophy," Henry Wood on "Thinking as a Fine Art," Bolton Hall on "Single Tax," Frederick Spier on "The Eight Hour Law," Eltweed Pomeroy on "Direct Legislation," Henry Blackwell on "Woman Suffrage," J. H. Hyslop on "Problems of Physiology," Booker T. Washington on "Tuskegee," Elihu Thomson on "Electricity of the Future," Cyrus F.

Brackett on "The Past and the Present Outlook of Electrical Science," Jacob Riis on "How the Other Half Lives."

Rare opportunities for help have been given along metaphysical lines by Charles Brodie Patterson, Horatio Dresser, Paul Tyner, Ellen M. Dyer, Emma Louise Nickerson, Helen Van-Anderson and others.

Who can forget Emerson Day in the Cathedral Pines! Frank B. Sanborn, the presiding officer, was the last resident member of the Concord School of Philosophy, and the friend and companion of Emerson and Thoreau. We sit about under the trees and listen to tender intimate touches from Emerson's life and experience. We hold his letters, written seventy years ago, in our hands. Then Charles Malloy gives a series of Emerson readings, with lines and interlines of interpretation, the wealth of a lifetime of study. The great tent is crowded Sunday afternoon with the people of the countryside to hear Edward Everett Hale. He gives us a mighty summing up of the reasons for peace, from the spiritual as well as from the historical standpoint. For three summers under a tree in the Lysekloster pines we have spent a morning with Joseph Jefferson in informal discussion. In the afternoon the tent is again crowded to hear him on "The Possibilities of the Drama," from the standpoint of a great actor.

One summer under these same pines Dharmapala, the Buddhist, pitched his tent; sometimes teaching from the platform, but more often from the door of his tent, a striking figure in his orange robe. Seventeen different faiths were represented that year at Greenacre. How times have changed since the good people—not many miles distant—heard in the dead of night the click of the horses' hoofs carrying their minister forty miles to Salem to be tried for witchcraft!

The Parliament of Religions, Sunday, August 30, 1897, was a notable occasion. The tent was crowded to overflowing, the sides wide open to the river and the fields. A platform beautifully decorated with pines was occupied by a remarkable group of persons: Miss Farmer, in the centre; Lewis G. Janes, presiding; Virchand R. Gandhi, representative of the Jains, in native violet dress and yellow turban; Charles Brodie Patterson of the broad school of mental science; Saradananda, the Vedantist, in the flame-colored robe and turban of his order, and by his side the Quaker, Edward Rawson; C. B. Young, Boston, and William A. Key, London, of the Unitarian church; Horatio Dresser, editor of the Journal of Practical Metaphysics; K. S. Guthrie of the Episcopal church; Paul Carus, editor of the Monist and Open Court, of Chicago; Jehanghier Cola in the white dress of the Parsee, representing Zoroastrianism; Mrs. Ole Bull, founder of the Cambridge Conferences; Alfred Martin, pastor of the free church of Tacoma, Washington, and Rabbis Fleischer and Berkowitz, of Philadelphia. The brilliant assembly, the picturesque colors, the scent of pine, the setting of river and meadow, the earnest, listening company, the few simple words of the speakers showing the essential unity of religion — all served to make an occasion not to be forgotten.

Although many charming circles have been formed in the farmhouses, the social life centers naturally about the Inn, where most of the lecturers have been entertained. There is simplicity of life, a charming absence of conventionality, an almost invariable recognition of the man apart from circumstances. Small circles meet on the piazza, along the river bank or in the meadows, discussing questions with the recognized leaders of thought. "And the people speak from their character, not from their tongue." When else could you hear, *without surprise*, in the momentary lull of a hotel dining-room?—"I do not know whether the spirits return to this earth, but I do know that progress is the law of the soul."

There are opportunities day after day for the individual to take his problem to the one best fitted to help him, and the personal contact has proved as great a factor in development as any words from the platform. Many a life of inaction has been awakened here into service. "In the light of greater lives we see the vision of our own."

In the fact that thousands have come to Greenacre, and thousands have been turned away for lack of accommodations, in the virility and force of the minds gathered here, in the questions discussed from the platform that affect the moral welfare and therefore the rational progress of the world—in the renewing of the individual, who, touched by the spirit, is born into a larger love for pushing starving humanity—in all this is demonstrated the need for such a centre in the social organism.

In a word, Greenacre can best be characterized as a *centre*. It is not an organization; it is not an institution, "the lengthened shadow of one man," but a great spiritual, formative *centre*, the trend of thought broadening with the need of the times.

The crucial test is therefore not a test of the value and purity of the ideal, but a test of methods and their practical application. Can a movement depending only upon voluntary aid live in the world to-day? Only last year a man died in London, who, during the last sixty years, has taken care of thousands of orphans. The money necessary to support this immense work was given unsolicited and used according to the strictest business principles. So far as Greenacre amalgamates with the highest ethical standards of the business world, the truth it stands for, just so far, "armed with the Sword of the Spirit," will it penetrate into the heart of the grossest materialism, and bring forth the willing tribute of an awakening spirit-loving service.

GREENACRE, *August, 1899.*

This year, 1900, marks the seventh season of the Greenacre Lecture Course. It was decided to make of it a Sabbatical year, a year of quiet rest, one in which to review the past and consider the future. Although no programs have been issued, there has been an average of three lectures a week, with a daily morning devotional, and an attendance of nearly nine hundred persons. Edward Everett Hale, Charles Brodie Patterson, Samuel Richard Fuller, Ralph Waldo Trine, Edward Cummings, Paul Tyner, Helen M. Cole, Lyman C. Newell, Ellen M. Dyer, R. C. Douglas, Swami Abhedananda, Fillmore Moore, Florence Richardson, Richard Ingalese, Jean du Buy, and Charles Malloy have spoken from the platform. A much needed rest has made necessary Miss Farmer's absence the last season.

1901 will undoubtedly mark a new era in the development of this movement: a movement which stands, let it be remembered, not for personality or place, but for life, for progress.

ANNA JOSEPHINE INGERSOLL.

GREENACRE, *September, 1900.*

www.ingramcontent.com/pod-product-compliance
Lightning Source LLC
Chambersburg PA
CBHW061317040426
42444CB00010B/2690